You're HIRED!
10 Tips to Rock Out Your Interview and Land Your Dream Job.

Copyright © 2017 by iRock Development Solutions, LLC

Publisher: UImpact Publishing Group

Editor: Cheryl Squalls

All Rights Reserved.

No part of this book may be used, reproduced, uploaded, presented, stored or introduced into a retrieval system, or transmitted in any way or by any means (including electronic, mechanical, recording, or otherwise), without the prior written permission of the author and publisher, with the exception of brief quotations for written reviews or articles referencing the author. No copying, uploading, or distribution of this book via the internet or any other means is permissible without the expressed written consent of iRock Development Solutions, LLC.

The author and publisher have made every effort to include accurate information and website addresses in this work at the time of publication, and assume no responsibility for changes, omissions, inaccuracies, or errors that occur before or after publication.

The publisher does not endorse or assume responsibility for the information, author, and writer websites, or third-party websites, or their content.

You're HIRED!
10 Tips to Rock Out Your Interview and Land Your Dream Job!

Business & Economics / Careers / Resumes

ISBN-10: 1975657020

ISBN-13: 978-1975657024

Dedications

My loving and supportive family – Irvin and Nadia who endured my stealing time away to write this book. I love you with all my heart.

My best friend and editor, Cheryl Squalls. Thank you for stealing time away from your family to be my second brain in writing this book.

My friends, colleagues, mentees, direct reports, and clients from whom my experiences and knowledge come from. May your careers be fulfilling as you continue your path to success.

My mentors and leaders, both past and present, who poured into me over the years. You helped shape me into the career professional I am today. You all were my inspiration to discover my true passion in developing others.

Last but not least, my cheerleader in heaven, my mother Nadine Maury Clark. I can hear you cheering me on saying "Go Nikki Go". I love you and miss you dearly.

Table of Contents

Introduction: So, Why Write This Book?

Chapter One
I got the interview! Now, what?.. 9

Chapter Two
Understand the Different Types of Interviews...................... 17

Chapter Three
Do's and Don'ts For a Successful Video Interview....................... 29

Chapter Four
Knowledge is Power: Study the Prospective Employer........... 37

Chapter Five
Dress to Impress: Yes, We Really Need to Talk About This..... 43

Chapter Six
Rock Your Opening Statement.. 51

Chapter Seven
Answer Interview Questions Using the iRock S.T.A.R Method..59

Chapter Eight
Rock Your Closing Statement.. 71

Chapter Nine
Interview Question Types and How to Answer Them 79

Chapter Ten
What to Do After the Interview……………………………. 91

Appendix
- Final Thoughts
- About the Author
- iRock Client Testimonials

Introduction

So Why Write This Book?

My success in helping job seekers understand their career potential resulted in increased self-confidence. This new-found confidence allowed them to navigate the muddy waters of career development to create a fulfilling career.

A fulfilling career included promotions, special projects, non-advertised opportunities, and higher pay. I truly believe to understand and own your value in the marketplace, you must articulate it properly in a résumé and powerfully in an interview.

The journey to write this book all began with a major company reorganization. With this reorganization came an exciting time of change and great opportunities.

I felt blessed to have a team to lead through this arduous change. Preparing direct reports, mentees, and even peers for career advancement was nothing new in my career. It was an expectation of my role as a leadership professional in the company. It was something I did as a byproduct of my day to day job. It was new for me because I had to prepare a large amount of people at one time. And I had to do it quickly in addition to my day to day duties.

I wrote internal résumés and cover letters, conducted mock interviews, and all the things in between to prepare direct reports, mentees, and even peers for promotional opportunities.

At the time, I had 11 direct reports. I promised I would not leave for another opportunity until I made sure they all promoted to new opportunities, if they so desired. One did not desire it as she was getting married and relocating to another city. All the rest, took me up on it. I'm excited to say, all 10 received promotions! The salary increases ranged from $5,000 to $14,000.

With my entire team promoted, I took on a new team. I helped two new direct reports, a few non-direct reports, and a mentee promote to the next level with my mentee promoting to leadership. All of this, including my 10 team members above, occurred within an eight-month period and while still doing my day to day job.

Word spread throughout the department. I began assisting more employees with their quest for promotions and other opportunities. The flood of requests was about to overtake my assigned role. It became overwhelming, so much so, I had to turn people away. But…. I simply loved it!

It was not until two of my direct reports approached me and strongly suggested I write résumés as a business. They said people would pay me to write their résumé and they would even hire me if they needed a job outside the company. I listened intently and said ok, I would think about it.

I never thought about writing résumés as a business. It was simply what I loved to do – help articulate a person's potential on paper and in person via interview prep. I have always been a good writer but I just never thought about using my writing skills and my love for people development as a business.

Well, I thought and prayed about it. To test the concept, I decided to post the results I achieved on the wonderful world of social media. I talked about the work I did on internal résumés and cover letters, and interview prep and the results I accomplished.

To my surprise and delight, direct reports I worked with throughout the company began to weigh in on how I assisted them in the past. They became my social proof of my ability to write a compelling career story and help others with their careers. Almost instantly, I began to get inbox requests asking how much would I charge to write their résumé. And as they say, the rest is history or should I say "herstory". iRock Development Solutions, LLC dba iRock Résumés was born and my prayer answered.

"You're HIRED!"
10 Tips to Rock Out Your Interview to Land Your Dream Job

Chapter One

"I got the interview! Now, what?"

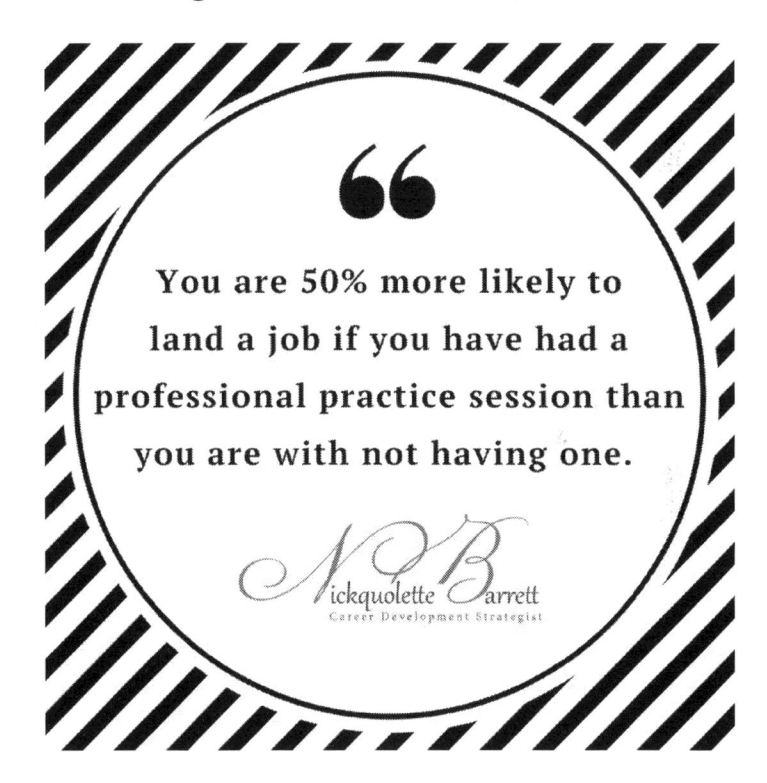

> You are 50% more likely to land a job if you have had a professional practice session than you are with not having one.
>
> *Nickquolette Barrett*
> Career Development Strategist

"I got the interview! Now, what?"

Congratulations! You put the tips from my book *"You're Hired! – Ten Ways to Rock Out Your Résumé to Land an Interview"* to good use! Good job!

Doesn't it feel good to finally get an interview? Yes! But wait – don't panic!

The mere mention of an interview can send the most confident person running with their hair on fire! But this does not have to be the case for you. Preparing for an interview, and well prepared, will help you ace it with flying colors.

You have the ability to rock out the interview just like you rocked out your résumé. The key is to not separate the two – the résumé from the interview.

What I mean by this statement is people send out résumés hoping, in and of itself, would be the way to get the job. And, this is what they expect after investing in a résumé prepared by a professional. Not so. The résumé is only the first step.

I know you are probably saying "like duh"! But trust me. Subconsciously, this is exactly what most job seekers think. They think *"Oh, I'll just send in an awesome résumé, and they'll call me for the job so they MUST want to hire me!"* Not so. Not that it can't happen. But the chances of it happening are slim to none.

As quick as you landed the interview, you could lose the job opportunity just as quick. How? By being unprepared, or flat out, having a bad interview. Or at least, one you are not happy with.

So, going in, please don't separate the interview as another entity. It goes hand in hand with a great résumé. The interview is a chance to discuss your résumé in more detail. The job of a résumé is to land the interview by telling a concise and compelling career story. Once you land the interview, you get a chance to tell the rest of the "story" behind the results and accomplishments chronicled in the résumé.

Please understand. The interview gets you one step closer to landing your dream job. It is the most important part of the entire job seeking process. But for some reason, people choose to "wing-it". I just don't get it. I really don't. I don't want you to do this. I want you to take it very seriously and prepare.

Let me break this down for you.

Companies invest up front time and resources to meet with you about your qualifications. You must make the same up-front investment into preparing for the discussion. If you don't even show up prepared and ready to rock the interview, why would they want you on their team? I know I wouldn't.

Consider This Scenario

Yay!! I got the "CALL" for the interview. My résumé finally got a response AND it's for the job I really want!

Then, reality sets in and a sense of fear and stress overcomes you.

Uh...oh.... I got an interview. Now what do I do? What do I wear? AND WHAT DO I SAY??? Oh well, I will be ok. I know how to talk to people.

Day of The Interview

Palms sweating.... pacing back and forth.... pacing forth and back.... Beads of sweat begin to form on the forehead......

tug This jacket must have shrunk.........

tick-tock.... tick-tock......

Interviewer: *Good afternoon Pat. We are ready for you.*

You're thinking: *We?? What do they mean by "we"?*

Enter the room and a scream goes off inside the head: *Oh noooo.... it's a panel with FIVE people!*

Heart pounding so loudly that it's deafening......mind racing.... pure fear rises up within.

15 – 20 minutes later

Interviewers: *Thanks for coming in Pat. We sure appreciate you taking time to come meet with us.*

And then you get the dreaded statement,

"We'll be in touch" with a half-smile and limp handshake.

Oh drats. I don't like that statement.

Day 1, 2, 3 go by......nothing....

Checking email.... checking for missed calls...... nothing.... just nothing.

Week 1, 2, and even 3 go by......nothing

Checked the mail about a few weeks later. Rejection letter with feedback comes in. You read it with horror and then sudden disappointment. The letter says your interview lacked depth. It also says you did not communicate the value you could bring to the role and to the company. They chose someone *"more qualified"*.

That someone more qualified, I bet, was someone who was prepared.

Does the scenario above sound like you? Do you struggle with articulating your value like Pat? Do you get stressed at the mere idea of having to go into an interview?

Well, having a practice session with a professional (preferably me) will help tremendously.

You are 50% more likely to land a job with a professional practice session than you are without.

The Old 5P Statement Still Holds True

Proper Preparation Prevents Poor Performance

In short, *"Practice makes perfect!"*

Let's look at it this way. If you are asking a potential employer to pay a decent salary plus benefits, do yourself a favor. Go in prepared to knock their socks off. If you don't take the time to prepare, it's a waste of time for you and the potential employer. It also shows you are not serious about the interview, the job, and worse yet, your career. This is not a good showing on your part.

Think about the interview as the only key to your dream job. The key to get you to the next step in your career. Don't take it lightly. Otherwise, the potential interviewer(s) won't take you seriously.

Here are some interview preparation tips to consider before we get into the meat of this book.

- **Have a great attitude and disposition.** Be sure to greet the interviewer(s) politely with a smile and a firm (not bone crushing) handshake. If you have small hands like me and wear a ring on your right hand, take it off to avoid having the ring crushed between your fingers (ouch! I personally know how this feels). In fact, don't even wear it.
- **Have an idea of your desired salary range.** Do this before conducting your job search. Research what a typical salary for the industry and role you are applying for. Weigh what you bring to the table against the salary norm and select a range you are comfortable

with. When asked in the interview, you will already have a reasonable salary range to work from.

- **Learn the art of salary negotiations.** Always begin the salary negotiation at the top of your range and work your way downward in small increments. Never begin at the bottom as you may be stuck there and unhappy. But, if you end up at the bottom of your range, be sure it's a bottom you are happy with.

  If you reach the bottom, ask for other perks. Perks can include additional vacation time, professional development time, a flexible schedule and the like. Believe it or not, you can ask for these accommodations if the company cannot meet your salary requirements. Only do this if the company is a good fit for you outside of the salary.

  Last but not least, support your salary request with reasons why you deserve it. Use facts, numerical results, education and training, etc. to back up the "why" behind the salary request. Doing this will make your request more solid and not just a wish.

- **Get some rest before the interview.** Yes, turn in early. The nerves may keep you up but if you must, drink a warm glass of milk to ease you into a peaceful sleep. Old remedy but still works wonders. I do not recommend sleep aids or even booze. Unfortunately, they may have an adverse effect on your ability to focus.

- **Confirm appointment time and location and allow extra travel time.** Do this before the interview date to avoid being late. Unforeseen circumstances like being held up in heavy traffic can and has happened. Take a test run around the same time and day of the week of your interview to ensure you have enough time to make it there. It's better to get there before time than on-time. Pay attention to the area so you remember what the area looks like the day of your interview.

Let me tell you a personal painful story.

I am directionally challenged. There. I said it. I have outed myself. I love and must have a global positioning system (GPS).

One time, I relied on my GPS to take me to an interview location. This is when GPS's were relatively new to the scene. The GPS led me to a dead end 45 minutes away from the correct location. Needless to say, I was now 15 minutes late to the interview even though I arrived at the incorrect location 30 minutes early.

Unfortunately, I was allowed to proceed with the interview. I say unfortunately because one of the interviewers was not happy at all and did not hide it in the least little bit. He expressed it with his body language and, worse yet, he expressed it verbally during the interview.

Talk about being uncomfortable with beads of sweat on my forehead and under my armpits. It was just awful. Absolutely awful. I still shutter when I think about it. Unfortunately, I lost out on a great opportunity I worked hard to prepare for. It was an unfortunate and hard lesson to learn. Hence, the tip to take a test run BEFORE the interview.

What are your fears of going into the interview?
In what ways can you overcome those fears?

_____

_____

_____

_____

_____

_____

_____

_____

_____

_____

_____

Chapter Two

Understand the Different Types of Interviews

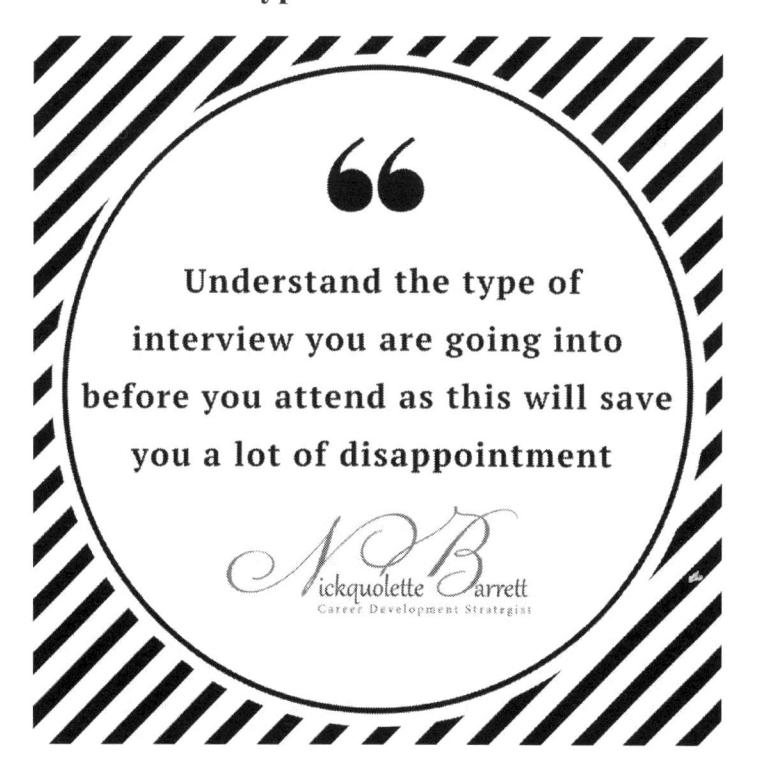

> " Understand the type of interview you are going into before you attend as this will save you a lot of disappointment

Nickquolette Barrett
Career Development Strategist

Understand the Different Types of Interviews

Before we get too far into the weeds about interviewing, I thought it would be helpful to understand the definition and meaning of an interview. Sometimes, getting a basic understanding can help us grasp a concept for what it truly is and not for what we think it is.

An interview is a conversation or a process by which a person or a group of people ask questions in order to gain more in-depth information about your skills and abilities.

Interviews can be formal or informal. Structured or unstructured. Or a combination. But how would you know?

When you land an interview, ask these questions.

1. What type of interview will it be? One on one or panel?
2. What are the names, positions, and titles of the interviewers? *(Note: Get the spelling of their names so you can prepare thank you letters in advance. More about this later).*
3. How long does the interview normally take?

Knowing these key facts will help you know, in advance, what to expect and how best to prepare. Even question number three is important as you want to make sure you structure your answers to include pertinent information you want the interviewer to know out there. For example, concise answers with a 30 minute or less interview. Or a slightly more in depth answer for an hour interview. All in all, knowing the type of interview is very important.

Let me tell you a story.

One of my interview prep clients had been out of the workforce for over 10 years. She was ready to re-enter the workforce. She applied for a position and got an interview. She had not prepared for the interview. She went in based on her assumption of how interviews "used" to be conducted.

To her surprise, when she walked into her very first interview after a 10-year absence from the workforce, it was with a panel. She had no idea what to do or how to deal with it. Unfortunately, she did not do well. And, you guessed it. She did not get the job and was quite disappointed.

It was at that very moment she realized she needed professional help and became my client. We talked about how companies have changed in how they interview candidates and panel interviewing is more common these days, than not. The reason being, panel interviews tend to be less biased and are great time savers.

To avoid a surprise like my client, become familiar and understand the different types of interviews. Understanding the different types is the beginning of being prepared and not being caught off guard like my client.

Following, are a few types of interviews and an explanation of what they mean, what to expect, and how you should prepare.

Types of Interviews

Telephone

A telephone interview can be either your foe or your friend. My goal for you and my clients is to make a phone interview your friend. Your best friend at that.

One of the ways recruiters narrow the candidate pool is by conducting a phone interview. This occurs after you've made the cut with a great résumé. At this stage, your job is to make it to the next phase – a face to face meeting with the hiring decision makers.

Recruiters use phone interviews to weed out those who cannot present themselves well over the phone. Knowing this, your ultimate goal is to get on the interview list. So, beware and prepare. Don't allow yourself to get cut. Ace it as if you are going into a conference room face to face.

The goal of the phone interview is to build a rapport and sell yourself over the phone. This is where your personality must show through. You need to WOW them. If you do this well, you win the prize. The prize is the coveted invitation to sit in front of the true decision makers.

Challenges to Overcome in A Phone Interview

There are challenges with a phone interview. The person on the other end of the phone cannot see:

1. your smile
2. your eyes for eye contact
3. your gestures to read your body language
4. and all the other things that go along with meeting someone in person

Another challenge is you can feel a sense of separation between you and the interviewer. You think to yourself *"I am a dynamic person when you meet me face to face – trust me, I truly am!!"* That's well and good. But, how will the person on the other end know?

Don't fret. All is not lost. You can have a successful phone interview if you follow these simple tips.

1. **Prepare.** Yes, even for a phone interview. You don't want to treat it any less than if you were sitting across the room from an individual. Have notes of your examples and your résumé in front of you. This will be one of the few times you can sort of "cheat" in an interview. However, be familiar with your examples and résumé so you do not rely on them holistically. You don't want to give the impression you are reading your response to the questions.

2. **Distractions are a no-no.** Eliminate background noise and distractions – i.e. television, people talking, children playing/crying, dogs barking, etc. Also, eliminate your own personal distractions. Yes, you know what they are – checking texts, social media or an email. Find a private and quiet place to conduct the interview. And, yes put away the computer. If you rely on it for your notes, print them instead and have them laid out in front of you. No distractions mean NO DISTRACTIONS.

3. **Call Initiator & Greeting.** When you receive the interview invitation, be sure you know who will initiate the call. If you are the call initiator, conduct a call test a day or two before to rule out technical difficulties. If the company representative will initiate the call, have a professional greeting prepared. Answer the phone and say something like this:

    "Hello, this is (place your name here)."

    "Hi. This is (interviewer's name) calling from (hiring company/organization)."

    "Hi [interviewer's name]. Thank you for taking the time to speak with me today."

    Doing this sets the proper tone for the interview. This could allow you to begin to win over the person on the other end. Remember, this is what you are striving for.

4. **Smile.** Yes, even though the interviewer may not be able to see your smile, they will be able to hear it. The "hearing the smile in your voice" phrase is very common in phone sales and customer service jobs. Companies thrive on this to continue to grow their businesses. When the recruiter hears your smile, this assures them that the company's clients will also. So, put on your best attitude and smile, smile, SMILE! Trust me. They are listening for it.

5. **Engage.** Engaging the interviewer with your personality will help bring them into your world. Speaking with intention and in a story format is essential. Think of it as if you are talking to a friend you haven't spoken to in a while and you have to catch them up on the latest. The trick is, you only have a few minutes to do it. Focus on telling your career story in a conversational and concise format. Don't ramble. Being concise will make it easier to hear, follow, and digest. And, most of all, it will be memorable.

6. **Breathe.** Talking too fast without taking a breath will give the impression that you are nervous and unprepared. Breathe as you speak. Sit up straight and speak at a moderate rate of speed. This gives the interviewer time to follow you and take notes.

7. **Social Queues.** Pay attention to social queues. Speaking too long will not give the interviewer a chance to respond or ask follow up questions. Remember. They are on a time limit. Since you can't see them, listen intently to make sure you are in sync with the interviewer. This eliminates rounding out your answer with a statement like *"Yeah, that's about it!"*. End with a strong queue to signal you are done speaking. Preferably, with a result from the example you just spoke about.

8. **Practice.** Practice a phone interview several times before the actual interview. Have a family member, friend, colleague, or mentor practice with you. They can give you feedback on the way you sound, if they hear your smile, hear your confidence, etc. But remember, as well meaning as friends and family may be, they are not professionals. They are limited in their scope of practice. Consider hiring a professional interview prep coach (preferably me). It will be well worth the investment.

9. **Be on time.** This should go without saying but timeliness is still judged for phone interviews. If you sound like you set up for the interview a

minute or two before, this will show your lack of preparation. Be in the room at least 15-30 minutes before time. Check everything to make sure its ready. Sit and wait just as if you were sitting in a room waiting for someone to come and escort you into a conference room. Doing this puts you into "interview" mode.

All in all, the phone interview may seem intimidating but it does not have to be if you prepare. And, just because it is a phone interview, does not mean it is any less important. So, practice, practice, practice so you can rock it out!

One on One

The most common type of interview is the traditional face to face interview. One interviewee with one interviewer.

Most people are comfortable with this type of interview as you can feel more in control. This control gives you the ability to focus on one person asking the question as opposed to several. You can also gauge the body language of one person so you know how to respond to the questions.

Challenges to Overcome in a One-on-One Interview

The challenge with a one-on-one interview is that the power is in the hands of one person. The interviewer can either like or dislike you which can be the difference in getting the job or not.

Some companies use this method as phases to their interview process. The goal is to past the *"test"* of the person conducting the one-on-one. If you past the test, you go on to the next phase which can either be another one-on-one or a panel interview.

To overcome these challenges, use the tips I gave for the phone interview.

- Prepare
- Smile

- Engage
- Breathe
- Social Queues
- Practice
- Be on time

Score Extra Points: Mimic the Interviewers Mannerisms

In addition, watch the interviewer's mannerisms. Are they expressive? Then mimic them and become expressive. Are they more reserved? Consider becoming more reserved than you are normally.

Watching the interviewer and mimicking them, is something no one thinks about. Use this to your advantage so you can score points. The underlining points could be *"hey, I kinda like this guy/gal."* Every brownie point can help elevate you over the competition.

Panel/Team

The name already gives a clue on this kind of interview. It involves anywhere from two to eight interviewers. For now, I will use the word "panel" instead of "team" to further our discussion.

The panel interview is used to save time by allowing more than one decision maker to assemble once. This is better than having several meetings with the same candidate lasting hours and/or days.

The panel interview also eliminates any biases during the selection process. It allows for a joint decision when choosing the best candidate for the job. Having several people weigh in allows for different viewpoints in making the final decision. This is sometimes a safer bet than a single person's point of view.

Challenges to Overcome in A Panel Interview

For the interviewee, a panel interview can:

1. be intimidating due to the number of people involved
2. be challenging due to having various individuals and personalities involved
3. have you repeating your answers so everyone can hear and write them down

To overcome these challenges, use these tips.

- Pay attention and engage more than one person in the room.

- Make eye contact with everyone in the room so no one feels slighted.

    o Making someone feel slighted can hurt your chance of gaining favor from that individual. Your job is to gain favor from each person in the room. The more votes in your favor, the better!
    o Eye contact also engages the panel making them more likely to write your answers down so you do not have to repeat them.
    o Discern who the biggest influencer is. Once known, end your answer looking at that person, with a confident smile.
    o Keep your answers in the iRock-S.T.A.R. format (discussed later). This will allow you to remember what you said a lot easier.
    o Thank all participants at the end of the interview. Address them by name with a firm, not bone crushing, handshake.

One-on-One versus Panel

When companies are looking for the best candidate, the most common interview types used are the one-on-one and the panel. There is much debate about which interview format is better. Whichever one a company chooses, it's your job to be ready.

The Interview Is a Tool To Get The Job

Like the résumé, an interview is the tool employers use to weed out candidates. Their goal is to select the best candidate for their company. You want to be that candidate!

Simply hearing about an available job is not enough. But working towards being the right person for the job is your goal. This can be achieved by accessing your strengths and weaknesses against the open position. The ability to understand your potential and know how to harness it will be key to acing the interview.

Your task is to be well prepared so you can go in with all the confidence in the world. Therefore, be ready to articulate your skills and achievements in a clear and concise manner. When you do this, you will have a greater chance to be chosen for the job.

Video

Video interviewing merits its own chapter. Turn the page to learn more.

What tips above are second nature to you? Which ones can you work on? Put a plan in place now, so when the time comes you are already half-way prepared for your upcoming interview.

_____

_____

_____

_____

_____

_____

_____

_____

_____

_____

Chapter Three

Do's and Don'ts for a Successful Video Interview

> "Video interviewing is quickly becoming a new phenomenon. Be prepared to conquer it.
>
> — *Nickquolette Barrett, Career Development Strategist*

Do's and Don'ts for a Successful Video Interview

Video interviewing is a means for companies to conduct interviews virtually. Communicating with co-workers via video or webcam is the new norm. Video conferences are in-person interactions allowing businesses to communicate when face-to-face meetings are not possible.

In our world of technology, video interviewing is becoming more and more popular. There are many virtual options available which allow the interviewer to interact with the job candidate. Unfortunately, it can also make the interviewing process a bit more difficult. But don't worry. I got you! I created an entire chapter on this topic because it is becoming a phenomenon quickly. Why? I'm glad you asked!

Video interviewing has gained immense popularity amongst employers because….

- It saves travel time for the interviewee.
- It saves time by eliminating the need to walk to meet the interviewee, walk to take them to the conference room, make formal introductions with handshakes, and anything else that normally goes with a face-to-face interview.
- More people can take part in a panel interview from different cities.
- It saves the potential employer travel expenses if the employer is in a different city or country.

Being successful in a video interview shows the potential employer you can communicate your thoughts and ideas on camera. In addition, they will have the opportunity to see your body language when dealing with a tough question. Being properly prepared to handle the video interview can be the key to your next opportunity.

For video interviews, there are some challenges you need to be aware of. I have listed below "do's" and "don'ts" to help you prepare to conquer the video interview experience. I will begin with the "do's" as it's always nice to begin in a positive manner.

Do

- **Prepare your answers.** Video interviewers will still ask the same tough questions as they would in a face to face interview. So, take some time to prepare your answers. Run through sample questions and answers several times before the interview. Practice makes perfect.

- **Be prepared ahead of time.** Think about handouts, résumés or other documents the interviewer may need. Send them via email before the interview begins.

- **Learn and understand your computer settings**. Understanding your computer settings and options for the webcam will be very important. Read the manual, watch a video, and/or look it up online. Do whatever it takes. Test the links the company sends before the day of the interview. This will save you time and much embarrassment.

- **Test your microphone.** Do this before the video interview. Test it by video conferencing a friend or family member. There is nothing worse than sharing an awesome answer to a question but no one hears it because the sound is unclear. And, you will have the unfortunate task of trying to remember the awesome answer you just gave.

- **Mute your computer's microphone**. Do this whenever you are not speaking. This will eliminate background noise which can be an annoying distraction. Worse yet, it can disrupt the flow of the interview. Just remember to turn it back on when you begin to speak so keep your finger close to the button.

- **Choose a room with good lighting.** Artificial or natural is ok. Videographers say side lighting is best so angle yourself to take advantage of this tip. Poor lighting can affect the tone of the interview as it becomes a visual distraction. Having nice lighting gives you an automatic positive disposition. You want the interviewer(s) to see your face and body language clearly. Turn on your webcam and practice different angels until you get the most flattering one. Write it down so you can remember.

- **Wear appropriate interview attire.** Remember, you are visible on a video interview so please, dress for it. Doing this alone may get you the job as most people may not even make the effort. Dress fully as you never know if you may have to stand up. You can always change after the interview.

- **Make sure the area is neat and clean.** And, make sure the decor in the area you plan to take the video interview is appropriate. If your room looks like a catch all room, either clean it or find a different room. This also includes your desk! Avoid having coffee mugs, dishes and trash in the vicinity of the camera view. Simply, get rid of it. A cluttered and unclean area says a lot about who you are as a person.

- **Look into the camera.** When it's time for you to speak, look into the camera instead of looking at yourself. I have to chuckle at this as I learned this first hand. Have you seen some of my early YouTube videos? Very entertaining to say the least. However, this is human nature. We naturally want to look at ourselves when talking on the computer screen. Refrain from doing this with all your might. If you catch yourself doing it, quickly correct it.

- **Treat the camera as if it were a person.** Look directly at the video camera when speaking. Maintain attention when listening to the interviewer. Looking away too often will make you appear distracted and uninterested. Also, be aware, some video conference services have a time delay. Be careful about speaking too soon because you do not want to interrupt the interviewer.

- **Be cautious of your body language and movements.** Don't look up to the ceiling when answering a question. Pretend as if it were a face-to-face interview so you don't seem anxious or unprepared on video. Unfold your arms and be mindful of unflattering body language. Practice by recording yourself and play it back. Eliminate anything unflattering.

Don't

- **Position your camera too low**. This can cause the interviewer(s) to see only your chest. I, and a panel, had the unfortunate horror of looking down a lady's blouse the entire interview. I have to wonder if it was intentional as I was the only female on the panel. Guess what? She did not get the job.

  On another note, don't set it too high where they can look up your nose. An awkward camera angle can be distracting and unflattering. Adjust your camera so it is eye level. Practice the perfect angle **BEFORE** the video call. Trust me on this one.

- **Risk wearing clothes only the top up.** Think about it. What if you have to stand up unexpectedly? How will it look if you have on shorts or worse yet, your underwear? Play it safe. Dress as if you were meeting the interviewer(s) at their office.

- **Check or read emails.** In fact, close all open screens on your computer. Only keep open the browser you will use for the video interview. Not a good look for a pop up of your high-school buddy saying something crass on your social media feed. Trust me. It happens. It's easy to tell if you are not focused and engaged during the interview. Be 100% engaged and present as this can be the difference of hearing ***"You're hired!"*** or not.

Overall, video interviewing is very similar to a regular face to face interview. Try not to stress or make yourself appear awkward on camera. Prepare, prepare, and prepare some more.

Make a checklist to ensure you cover all the basis before the video interview.

Chapter Four

Knowledge is Power:
Study the Prospective Employer

> "You need to interview the company just as much as they are interviewing you"
>
> — Nickquolette Barrett, Career Development Strategist

Knowledge is Power: Study the Prospective Employer

Knowledge is power. The ability to use information to gain access into whatever job you desire can help the interviewing process.

One of the ways to be confident in any interview is to know the company in which you wish to land a job. Take the time to research the company. This will help you understand the company's background and culture.

When going into an interview, be familiar with the company's:

- Vision and mission statement
- The date when and where the company was established
- The product and/or services they render
- Their philanthropic efforts
- What makes them unique and different from their competitors
- The names of the board of trustees, the managing director, etc.

Doing the above, will not only make you feel prepared, but more confident. In addition, you will be seen as a job candidate who has done their homework in getting to know their company.

Another way to think of researching a company, is to think of it as if you are interviewing the company. You need to interview the company just as much as they are interviewing you. Why? Because during your research you may find the company is not a good fit for you.

Hmmmm......imagine that. Yes, it's true and it can happen.

Further Preparation for Your Own Comfort

- **Know the company's financial strength.** Knowing this information will help you avoid the chopping block if job cuts arise. Don't put yourself in harm's way. You can find out the financial health of a company by putting the company's name and the phrase "financial strength" in your search engine.

- **Know the company's reputation and any leader within.** If the company's reputation does not line up with your values, you may want to pass on the interview. Same goes for the leaders within the company.

- **Understand the company culture.** Again, does it line up with your values? Can you embrace and conform to it? Going in and attempting to change it will be the wrong attitude. Remember, it's their company and they get to choose how they operate.

- **Understand the field and how companies operate and compete therein.** Having this understanding going it, can separate you from the competition. You will want to articulate you can and will do your part to help them stay competitive. And, understanding the "how" will give you a leg up over the competition.

- **Reach out to a current employee.** This adds further credibility to your employer research. It could either seal the deal or repel you basd on the inside details the employee gives on the company, department, and job.

A way to find someone at the intended company, is to search LinkedIn's database (assuming you are on LinkedIn. If you are not, get on it fast!) Send an in-mail asking to have a brief 15-minute conversation about the company, the deparment, and open job oppotunity. Stay within your 15 minutes to be respectful of the person's time. Cut it off at 13 minutes if possible.

What if The Job is Not a Good Fit?

As stated, there can be a hard reality that after your research of the job and/or company, you may find you are no longer interested. It's ok. It happens. You may have saved yourself a lot of heartached. If this happens to you, you can either cancel the interview or go through with it. Choosing the later will give you the option of making your final determination afterwards.

If you decide to go through with it, pay attention as there could be signs that taking the job could be a bad move. Even though you may need to make a move, sometimes taking a job that is not a good fit may be worse than having no job at all.

The tell-tell signs to look out for are:

- The salary is extremely high
- The culture is off or appears unreal
- Inconsistent expectations of the role from the recruiter to the interviewer
- The environment feels cold and uncomfortable
- Your potential peers seem stand-offish, rude and unwelcoming

On a Positive Note

The interview process is about the company learning about you as you learn about them. You may find you have found your dream job and none of the items on the list above exist. If this is the case, go for it with all you might! I will be cheering you along the way!

What do you know about the company(ies) you are interviewing with? List it here.

_____

_____

_____

_____

_____

_____

_____

_____

_____

_____

_____

What are the pros and cons of the company you are interviewing for? What do you like about them? What don't you like?

_____

_____

_____

_____

_____

_____

_____

_____

_____

_____

Chapter Five

Dress to Impress
(Yes, we really need to talk about this)

> "Don't just dress for the interview. Dress for your self-confidence.

Nickquolette Barrett
Career Development Strategist

Dress to Impress *(Yes, we really need to talk about this)*

How you present yourself in your attire is important. There is a popular saying that says:

The way a man (or woman) is dressed is the way he(she) will be addressed.

This is a powerful statement. Your style of dressing says a lot about you as a person. It also says a lot about your understanding of the job you are seeking. One of the best weapons in your arsenal is your interview attire.

In job hunting, making a good first impression is extremely important. Like the saying goes, *"you only have one chance to make a good first impression"*. If you are at all serious about your career, then dress like it.

The product you are marketing to a potential employer is your skills and abilities. Your dress enhances your marketing. It is like the packaging on a product. If the packaging is good, it attacts a potential buyer. Your attire should do the same in attracting a job. It should indicate that you are ready to work the same day of the interview. Who knows? They may have you do just that. In fact, this happened to me when I pounded the pavement to find my own college internship. The owner of a Spanish newspaper took one look at me after I made my inquiry speech and put me to work the same day! I loved it!

An interviewer immediately observes your attire. From their first observation, they can often pre-determine if you are a viable candidate. This is a true fact. Your appearance can make or break an opportunity for you. People are visual creatures. The eyes tell the brain how to think. If your appearance is all wrong. The eyes will tell the interviewer(s) brain that you are all wrong for the job.

Dress for Self-Confidence

Do yourself a favor. Dress for not only the interview. Dress for your own self confidence.

The fact is, when you are well dressed, you feel well. And when you feel well, you feel confident. Your self-esteem increases and you become confident in speaking with the interviewer. Thus, when planning your attire, wear something that reflects professionalism and confidence. It should also display your ability to fit in with company culture (remember this during your research).

A mentee once asked if they should dress professionally for their interview or dress business casual like the company culture. I asked, *"Do you want the job?"* The person answered, *"yes"*. I replied, *"Then dress like you want it"*. *"As a matter of fact, dress like you want the bosses job!"*

What's behind this advice? Nowadays, many companies are not only interviewing for today. They are also seeking candidates to fill positions for tomorrow. This is called "succession planning" which is a process for identifying and developing new leaders who can replace leaders when they leave, retire or die.

Baby boomers are retiring and leaving companies at a rapid rate. This in turn leaves a shortage of candidates for key roles such as leadership/management positions. Don't short yourself on one of these opportunities. Look the part. And when you get the job, continue to dress like you want to advance in your career.

Here is what I recommend in general for men and women:

- Ensure attire fits well, is clean, and pressed
- Choose basic colors – navy, black, grey, neutral
- Wear polished shoes in black, navy, brown, or neutral
- White blouse/shirt – long sleeves are a plus

- Cover tattoos (as much as possible)
- Manicured hands – yes, even men – basic manicures are inexpensive or just do it yourself
- No nose and tongue rings
- Minimize or eliminate cologne or perfume *(Hint: you are not going on a date.)*

Of course, these are recommendations for company's who have a standard dress policy. If unsure, do your research. Reach out to a current company employee and ask what is or is not acceptable. They will give you an insiders viewpoint. Of course, always lean on the professional side regardless of what your research turns up. Professional attire is always the safest.

Gender Specific Recommendations

Listed below, I outlined gender specific recommendations. Again, these are just recommendations – but strong recommendations. They are based on my years of interviewing candidates. However, feel free to adjust as you see fit.

Women

- ✓ Wear closed toe with a modest heel no matter how in fashion open-toed and 4-inch heel shoes are.
- ✓ If you choose a suit with a skirt, make sure the skirt hem is below the knees allowing for a comfortable rise when you sit.
- ✓ If you opt for a pant suit, make sure it fits well and not too fitting or too tight. A tailored look is a neat and clean look.
- ✓ Wear a statement necklace and simple, non-dangling earrings.

- ✓ Do not wear clanking bracelets, especially if you talk with your hands. It's noisy and a huge distraction.
- ✓ Wear simple makeup. Stay away from bright lipsticks and heavy eyeshadow to avoid sending the wrong message. Neutral always wins.
- ✓ Wear a simple hairstyle. Do not have hair in your face. If you have a modern hairstyle with a long bang, pin it back. The goal is to let them see your eyes and full face.

Men

- ✓ Wear a suit or suit jacket with trousers.
- ✓ Wear a belt if you have belt loops on your pants. The belt should complement your shoes.
- ✓ No earrings. (Yes – men, leave them at home)
- ✓ Wear a tie with a pop of color but not too much. A little red is always nice. (Think presidential)
- ✓ Be clean shaven or neatly trimmed facial hair (this has become more acceptable)
- ✓ Invest in a fresh and clean haircut. If you wear your hair long, make sure they can your eyes and face.

Take the suggestions above to heart. If you do, the interviewer(s) will focus on what you are saying and not the distraction of your appearance. There's nothing against individuality. You can express your individual style AFTER you get the job and when the time is right. Don't give the interviewers any reason to turn you off before you get started. How you present yourself is totally in your control.

Know the Typical Dress Attire of The Company

Warning. After you land the job, make sure you align your style within the boundaries of the company's culture. So, before you apply, research the company's culture and dress code. From your research, you can determine if you are willing to conform. If not, don't apply as it could be a source of stress for both sides and even result in your dismissal.

I have another funny story for you.

During a panel interview I was a part of, a candidate came with a visible tongue ring. I must confess, it was a huge distraction. The only thing we could focus on during the entire interview was the tongue ring. It kept bobbing up and down as the candidate spoke. We could barely understand what she was saying.

What made matters worse, the attire was also unprofessional. Unfortunately, not one interviewer on the panel could remember the candidate's qualifications. We were distracted by the large tongue ring bobbing up and down and her appearance.

The entire panel was in disbelief. Why didn't the person remove it just for the 45-minute interview? The position they applied for required an element of customer facing. Having a tongue ring to conduct the company's business was unacceptable. Again, this was the company's culture. I don't have anything against tongue rings. I do have something against not being able to focus on the answers due to a distraction. In this case, it just happened to be a tongue ring.

Needless to say, the candidate did not get the job. Now this is not the worst part. This was an internal candidate interview which means the candidate and their manager should have known better.

The candidate's manager solicited feedback on why her employee did not get the job. I told her about the distraction of the tongue ring. The manager apologized and stated they forgot to tell the candidate to take it out before the interview. Wow…….enough said. Like manager, like employee…….and I digress……smh…

Now, I know some of you may think this was unfair and we were passing judgment. To be honest, we who are in the position to hire someone, don't care. We have a company brand to protect. It's not about us. It's about the one who signs our paychecks. It's our responsibility to find the best candidate to fit the company's culture and do the job.

In this case, the job was a customer service job – face to face and over the phone. The customer will need to understand the individual. It's the candidate's responsibility to market and present themselves as a professional. Not ours to weed through the mayhem to recognize they are a professional in hopes they won't wear the tongue ring while answering a customer's call or meeting them face to face.

I apologize for the bluntness, but it's true. Society is changing to be more accepting in certain areas, but not as fast in corporate America. And, yes. There are companies who may be ok with totally relaxed attire, visible tattoos, tongue rings and the like. Seek those out if they are more in line with who you are. Doing so will cause less stress on you and the company. Unfortunately, some companies are just not there yet. Corporate America is changing but just a little slower than society.

Ok. Off my soap box and back to proper dressing. When you pay attention to your appearance, the interviewer will see you as a conscientious employee. It also shows you believe in your personal brand and the company you want to be associated with.

Dressing impeccable for an interview does not have to cost a bundle. You can find great pieces at your neighborhood consignment or thrift store. Shop around as you might be surprised as what you might find. This is coming from someone who thrifts. I have found great pieces for a fraction of the retail price. Try them and make sure you let me know what you find!

Take a look at your wardrobe. What's missing? What do you need to purchase? List the items needed here.

_____

_____

_____

_____

_____

_____

_____

_____

_____

_____

_____

_____

Chapter Six

Rock Out Your Opening Statement

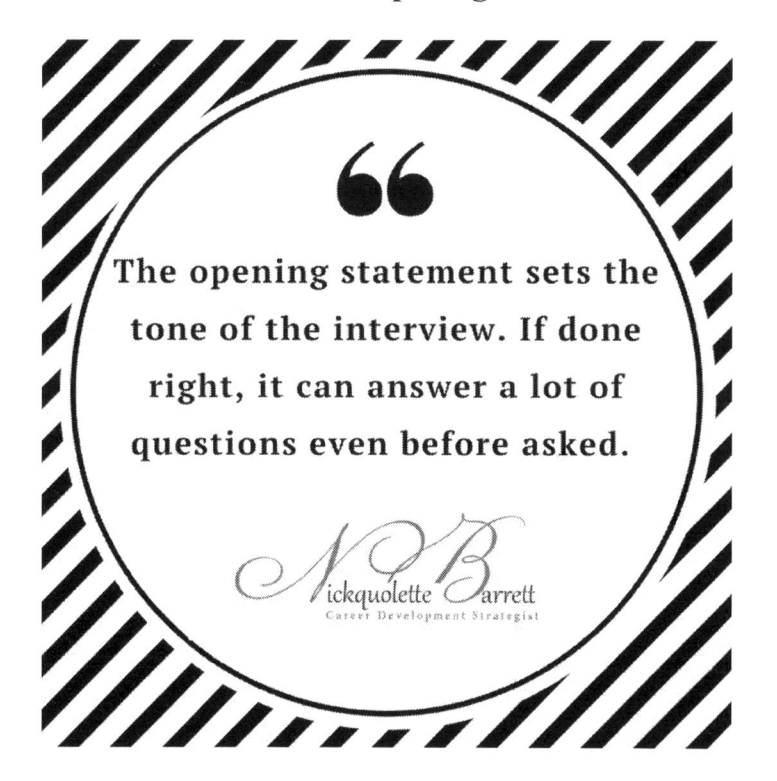

> "The opening statement sets the tone of the interview. If done right, it can answer a lot of questions even before asked."
>
> — Nickquolette Barrett, Career Development Strategist

Rock Out Your Opening Statement

The opening statement sets the tone of the interview. It gives the interviewer(s) an overview of who you are as a professional and as a person. If done right, it can answer a lot of questions even before asked.

What is an opening statement? An opening statement is like an attorney's opening statement in a trial. The attorney sets the stage for the jurors. She introduces the core facts of the case all while doing it in a persuasive manner. She also provides a general outline of what to expect during the trial. In essence, the attorney uses the opening statement to secure the interest of the jury to bring them into her camp. And if it is strong and compelling, it will grab the full attention of the jury right out of the gate.

You as an interviewee will need to do the same as the attorney above. This is your chance to state your case in a compelling and persuasive manner. Be ready to articulate your skills, abilities, and talents in the best light possible. The goal is to win the full attention of the interviewer(s) and to bring them into your camp right at the start.

The key to a great opening statement is to NOT regurgitate your entire résumé. Remember, they have it in front of them. And, the majority of the time, they have reviewed it. If not, they will ask you to go through your job history as an interview question. So, prepare your response just in case. Just don't give it without being asked.

The opening statement is your chance to make a great first impression. Come out with the big guns by highlighting three to four of your most powerful competencies. Choose ones that aligns with the job you are applying for. It's a great way to bring overlooked information in the résumé to their attention.

Having a great opening statement is your opportunity to define yourself on your terms. The stronger and more compelling, the less probing the follow up questions will be.

Don't snooze on the opportunity to prepare an awesome opening statement. And, please don't wing it. It has the power to set the stage for an awesome interview session.

Points to Consider and Remember

Consider and remember these points as you prepare your opening statement.

- Most interviews are won or lost on the competency of the opening statement.
- Keep it concise like an elevator pitch. Make it 60 to 120 seconds max. Any longer, the interviewers may lose interest.
- Think of three to four strong statements that align with the job opening. Getting these out, up front, will immediately show you as a qualified and viable candidate.
- Secure the interest but keep it light and engaging.
- Make good eye contact with the interviewer and everyone in the room if there is a panel.
- If you use a lot of filler words such as "um, uh, err, ah, like, okay, right, and you know" on a daily basis, be sure to eliminate them. It will weaken what you have say.

End on a Personal Note

End the opening statement by highlighting something personal about yourself. Some people may underestimate the value of this. They may even question *"why would interviewers need to know my personal business?"* Remember, interviewers are people too. People connect on a professional *and* a personal level. Let them see you are an all-around great person, both professionally and personally.

Here are a couple of examples of great personal endings to an opening statement.

"I am a big fan of the (insert sports team here), love to read, and I am awesome on the bar-be-que grill. My steaks are always cooked perfectly."

Or

"I love to line dance, watch old movies, and make my award-winning banana pudding!"

Give them a big smile after saying something like the above.

Now how are those for an ending to an opening statement. Wouldn't they make you like the person? Or at least want to go to their house for dinner. Sure, it does!

The value of ending the opening statement with a personal statement:

1. Brings the interviewers into your world. It could most likely stir up conversation outside of the interview questions. This will build rapport.
2. It takes the tension out of the room and allows you to feel more relaxed.
3. Allows the interviewer(s) to see you as a real person and give a glimpse into your personality. This will enable them to envision you as a part of the team/group/organization.
4. Ensures the interviewer(s) remember you.

I have included two examples of opening statements I wrote for my clients at the end of this chapter.

One of the clients interviewed for a director level opportunity at the company she worked for. Since this was a very experienced and accomplished leadership professional, I wanted to make sure she came out the gate swinging with a high-level overview of what she had to offer. She absolutely loved what I wrote.

Feel free to model yours after this. It does not have to be as long. It depends on what level of opportunity you are applying for.

The second one I wrote was for a client who had been out of a job for over a year. A former client referred her to me. This opening statement is a good one to model yours after as well. The good news is, the client went through my entire interview prep process and got the job!! Score!! She totally rocked it!

Opening Statement:

Interviewing Panel: Well, iRock Client, tell me a little bit about yourself.

iRock Client: I'd be happy to! But before I do, I would like to take this opportunity to thank you for meeting with me. It's my goal to make sure you all are glad you did. I say that because this opportunity is like a dream come true. I have been preparing myself for years to fulfill a role like this and it could have not come at a better time in my career.

The (name of job applying for) role will not only enable me to use my experience in underwriting, systems, and Agency – but will also allow me to leverage the relationships I've built in those business areas over the years. I understand the importance of collaboration to reach department and company goals. I have been in the trenches working and leading projects that relied on collaboration.

My current Agency experience has given me a holistic view of the company. It has allowed me to elevate my business acumen giving me a deeper understanding of this company. It was like that "ah-ha" moment when all the dots began to connect allowing me to see the big picture. I have been able to take this experience, add it to my prior experience to drive results.

In addition, I am a continuous learner. I am engaged in mentoring and make a concerted effort to understand our business. I am also an active member in various internal and external organizations.

I have a strong work ethic. I understand the value of being a team player, being coachable, and being resourceful all while being flexible and adaptable to competing, demanding, and changing needs.

In essence, I am –

1. A leadership professional with the ability to see a vision, help others see it, and the willingness to work to make it a reality
2. A person that thrives off relationships creating win-wins and effective collaborations
3. A good steward over what this company has allowed me the privilege to oversee in various roles and instilling that in the leaders I have the privilege to lead.

On a personal note.....

- I am a Chicago Sports team fan – I love the Bears and the Cubs.
- I love to travel – Maui is by far my favorite place to visit.
- I enjoy visiting National parks, spending time with family & friends, cross word puzzles & Sudoku as they keep my mind sharp.
- Lastly, my husband is a project manager in the systems department. We have a beautiful daughter name Lauren who is 14 months.

Again, thanks for meeting with me today.

P.O. Box 631562 Richardson, TX 75063 | 469-686-0753 | www.irockresumes.com | irock@irockresumes.com

Opening:

Question: Well, iRock client, tell me a little bit about you.

You: I'd be happy to but before that, I would like to take this opportunity to thank you for selecting me to meet with you all about this position. It's my goal to make sure you all are glad you did. I was pretty excited to get the call.

I pride myself on putting 110% into every job and/or task that I take on. I like a challenge and more importantly, I like finding ways to overcome challenges as well. I do this by not only drawing on my past experiences, I also do this by ensuring I use my resources – people, paper, and/or company electronic resources.

I'd like to also say that I have a great work ethic. I truly understand the value of not only being at work, but also being engaged in my work. I have had many opportunities to fill in for my managers because of it.

Last but certainly not least I am great at building relationships, which translates into my being a great team player. I enjoy collaborating with others as we focus on achieving a goal or goals. I value others strengths and capabilities and bring my own strengths and capabilities of research, accuracy, time management, and organizational skills to the table. I am an accounts payable whiz, have great learning agility, and am flexible.

On a personal note, *(fill in a few personal tidbits you feel comfortable sharing – i.e. marital status, children, pets, favorite sports team, hobbies, etc. – make it something you think will drum up a conversation)*

Again, thanks for meeting with me today.

Write a rough draft of your opening statement. The draft can be tweaked to fit each opportunity you are interviewing for.

Chapter Seven

Answer Interview Questions Using My iRock S.T.A.R Method™

> "Tell your career story in a concise, powerful, and impactful way."
>
> — *Nickquolette Barrett*, Career Development Strategist

Answer Interview Questions Using My iRock S.T.A.R. Method™

*(Please note: The **iRock S.T.A.R. Method**™, or any resemblance and/or likeness, is prohibited without the expressed written consent and/or licensing from iRock Development Solutions, LLC. This method is proprietary and legal action will be taken if used without written consent. Contact us for licensing of the method.)*

This chapter may be one of the longest chapters in the book. But, I promise you, it will be one of the most powerful for your job search strategy. That is, if you use it.

We have already established that researching the company, arriving on time, and appropriate attire sets the tone for the interview. We now need to establish what you will actually say in the interview so you can land the job.

The crux of an interview is having experiences, both past and present, you can draw from to answer the toughest interview questions. Winging an interview is a waste of your time and the interviewer(s) time. Your preparation needs to goes well beyond getting rest and dressing the part.

The key to getting your answers out concisely, orderly, and with depth will be to have an easy to follow format. I created a method to help you do this. It's called **iRock S.T.A.R. Method**™.

This method is a twist on the tried and true S.T.A.R. method which works but not as well as it could. The **iRock S.T.A.R. Method**™ can help you answer the most challenging interview questions with ease. Below are some things you need to do to prepare to use the **iRock S.T.A.R. Method**™ effectively. The method will be explained later.

Create a "Bank" of Interview Answers

What do I mean by "bank"? A bank is a list of experiences, achievements, accomplishments, lessons learned, lessons taught, etc. that make up your work and life experiences. Our day to day lives gives us many opportunities to learn, teach, grow, and more. With these experiences, we can create a "bank" of potential answers for interview questions.

"But I don't have a lot of experiences."

Bologna. All of us do. Get rid of the myth that interview answers have to come from work experiences only. Answers can come from a variety of places. It's the way you solved, overcame, taught, coached and/or developed others, etc. that make the difference.

Therefore, think long and hard. Conduct a brain dump as you think through your experiences. Make a list of past experiences from every area of your life. Write them down – big and small. The more recent experiences, place a star by them so you can provide both past and present answers.

The experiences can come from:

- work projects
- volunteering
- church activities
- kudos from team mates and/or management
- special projects outside of your normal day to day tasks
- committee work/projects from work, school, or professional organizations
- school projects
- job performance appraisals
- challenging and/or difficult customers
- challenging and/or difficult projects
- training, coaching, or mentoring opportunities
- your part in project collaboration
- the result of your achieving and/or exceeding team, departmental, or company goals

- any other significant achievements or results in your career or in school as a recent grad

The above list will can get you started. Creating a list like this can provide you a "bank" of answers to potential interview questions. Having a bank of examples allows you to plan your answers to fit almost any question asked. Always choose the best of the best of your bank. Eliminate the week ones, if necessary.

Core Competency – What is it what does it mean?

*If you think you can do it that's **Confidence**. If you do it, that's **Competence**. – Morris Code*

First, let's define what a competency is.

It is the ability to do something successfully or efficiently. A core competency is a defined level of competence in a job using a skill or skills.

We are all competent at something. However, we are more competent in some areas than others. Those areas become our core competency(ies). Core competencies are usually "must haves" listed in job postings to ensure they attract and hire candidates who can perform the job and perform it well.

Some core competencies can include:

- Team player/Teamwork
- Collaboration
- Research
- Resourceful
- Adaptable/Flexible
- Coachable/coaching
- Leadership
- Time management skills
- Organizational skills
- Adaptable

Most of us demonstrate, or have demonstrated, these competencies in one way or another. For example, you do not have to be a manager to show you are a leader. True leadership does not carry a title – it is a state of mind and the essence of who someone is. This could be you.

Align Competencies with Your Answers

Next, take the list of experiences you created and identify which competencies you used. It's ok to have more than one competency. The goal is to list the answers under the corresponding competency. This will give you the basis to choose your answers based on the competencies listed in the job posting.

Once you have your bank of answers developed, write each answer in a bullet point format. The reason for the bullet point format is so you can pick and choose the key points needed for the different competencies. Again, use the competencies you find in the job application to tweak your answers as needed.

The neat thing is, most jobs are looking for the same core competencies. Therefore, this should not be a hard task. But, trust me. It's a task that can elevate your preparation to rock star status!

Now the secret sauce to landing the job.

.....*dum-de-dum…dum…dummmmm (can't you hear the music).*

iRock S.T.A.R. Method™ Revealed

Now that you have developed your "bank" of interview question examples, let's formulate them into concise, orderly, and with depth reponses as promised at the beginning of this chapter. Using this method will allow you to breeze through your answers with confidence.

Take each one of your already written answers and use this format to give them structure. Use the bullet point format as it is a lot easier to remember than in sentence format.

Most everyone is familiar with the S.T.A.R. or the S.A.R. format. But why add an "iRock" in front of it? In all of my years of interviewing candidates, I found most people get lost in their answers using these formats. They seem to never to get to the result of their actions. Could it have been nerves? Maybe. Could it be because they were not able to maximize the S.T.A.R. format? I definitely say yes.

So, I said to myself, *"Self – why not add an "R" in front of the format?"* By adding an "R" in front if the S.T.A.R. method, it became my newly created **iRock S.T.A.R. Method**™. This method resolved the problem of interviewees forgetting to state result after telling the story or situation. The thought behind it is the candidate has a better chance of stating the result first and then build the story around it. This method allows the interviewers to write down the result of the answer if nothing else. The result is what they are listening for. This method ensures you give it to them.

The beauty of using the **iRock S.T.A.R. Method**™ is when they go back to their notes upon reviewing the candidates, they will have the notes of a client who was able to convey a result from the questions posed. Stating answers in the the **iRock S.T.A.R. Method**™ format will also be unconventional and memorable. It's all about elevating you above the competition. The interview is the most important phase of the job search. Let's make it count!

I have tested this method in my personal interviews and have gotten several jobs from it. The few I did not get the interviewers said I did well, but the other person had more experience for the role. But, hey. It happens.

I have also tested it with mentees and direct reports and they all got the job as well. And, I have tested it with my clients and the majority of them got their jobs too! With these great results, I decided to trademark this method because it really works! Score!!

Now let me break each area down on how you should formulate your answers from your "bank". Turn to the next page.

R is for Results

This is the juice of the entire **iRock S.T.A.R. Method™**. Here you will want to lead off your answer with an impactful result from the bank of examples you created. It can be from an improvement you made, a metric you achieved, a problem you solved, or the like.

Leading with a great result will perk up the ears of the interviewer grabbing their attention. They will become interested in the "how" of the achieved result. And, it will be the first thing they write down and see when they go back to review their notes.

Beginning with a great result is a benefit because:

1. It will be the first thing on the paper even if the interviewer did not write anything else
2. It will keep you focused on telling how you got the result without getting lost in your answer
3. It will set the tone for an impactful and memorable answer

S is for Situation/Scenario/Story

This is the situation, scenario, or story that best fit the question posed. After telling the result, tell the story to support it.

When brainstorming your story, choose the best of the story. Focus on the meat and leave out the fluff. Keeping it concise makes it stick in the interviewers' mind.

Once you have written out the story, write it again as two to three bullet phrases so it is easy to remember. Make it easy on yourself. Don't write it as a paragraph. Trying to remember a paragraph would be difficult. I always say, work smarter and not harder. However, if you can remember short paragraphs, then knock yourself out.

T is for Tasks

Don't get the story confused with the tasks you took to achieve the result. They are totally different. The story sets up the "why" you achieved the result. The "tasks" sets up the "steps" you took to achieve the result.

State two to three impactful tasks conducted to address the situation. Stay away from mundane tasks like "I made the copies". Who cares? Only speak of the high-level tasks you performed to achieve the end result. Always think detailed high-level activities. Not low-level meaningless tasks.

A is for Actions

Actions are similar to tasks, but not exactly. Actions tell of the "how" you achieved the result.

For example. A task may be "I developed a plan" which is a "step". The action may be "I gathered the team together to execute the plan" which is the "how".

Here, like in tasks, state two to three impactful actions you took to achieve the result.

R is for Results

This is the icing on the cake. This is an opportunity to re-inforce the result(s) you achieved from the situation/scenario/story above.

The key here is to re-state the result but different from how you stated it at the beginning of your answer. Make sure it is concise and with more emphasis by using carefully chosen power words. And when you say it, say it with an "as a matter of fact" confident (not braggadocios) attitude. This will give more "oomph" to your answer. Flash a nice confident smile once you say it. This will get you extra mileage with the interviewer(s).

Here are a few examples of using the **iRock S.T.A.R. Method**™ I used with my clients. They are written in a conversational style and not in an essay or book style.

1. Tell me about a difficult or complex idea you had to explain to someone. How did you communicate it? What was your approach? How did you ensure the person understood what you explained?

a. Competency: Communication – Express ideas and facts effectively, contributes to open exchange of ideas, and exhibits an understanding of audience needs.

iRock S.T.A.R. Method™

R: I was instrumental in the promotion of a new employee due her ability to successfully apply the concepts I trained and coached her on as it related to the complexities of the gift card process.

S: I was challenged to train a new employee on the complex gift card process which is more complicated than most people think. It's challenging because it is very technical as we use UPCS, barcodes, and IT POS integration. There are also a host of regulations that come up periodically so you have to stay up to date to advert any legalities.

T: The first thing that I did was develop a listing called "daily responsibilities of gift cards". It included 21 important steps from understanding contracts to setting up ad spots for the Sunday ad magazines. Other topics included launching new designed products and working with IT to get cards set up in our systems. The most difficult part was the UPC set ups with IT and how cards turned into live cards from set up to being sold in the stores.

A: I explained to the new employee each topic and the importance behind it. To ensure she understood, I used examples, asked her to take good notes, and walked her through each of the systems. I also gave examples of what could go wrong and how to avert potential risk. I provided copies of everything and used a real-life story to support each example. This aided in her ability to remember the concepts. By giving her real examples, and walking her through the system requirements, helped her to understand the process and the why behind the process more thoroughly.

R: The result, she became one of the top employees in department shortly afterward and was promoted to the responsibility of working on a new and larger gift card project.

1. **There are times where there is an incredible amount of data and information to be analyzed. Tell me about a time you faced this situation and exactly what you did to break everything down to what was most important.**

a. Competency: Critical Thinking – The ability to understand an idea, situation, or problem through an in-depth analysis.

iRock S.T.A.R. Method™

R: I reviewed data and conducted quality checks with our store design and planogram teams to ensure that the reset process ran correctly. Doing this allowed product to be delivered to 8000+ stores correctly which resulted in several millions of dollars in sales and profit.

S: Within the company, it is very important to ensure stores receive the right planograms in order to be able to setup the gift card displays correctly in all stores and with different store formats. The stores rely on corporate to provide correct instructions as a successful reset could result in millions of dollars of sales and profitability.

T: One of my day to day responsibilities was to work with the planograms and resets for gift cards which occurred three times/year. At that time, I had to review data for 100 different types of gift cards inclusive of the sales and the profit and margins.

A: After the review, I identified which cards were most profitable and which were underperforming. In addition, I would review that same information for regional cards to ensure they were mapped correctly to over 50 states. This entailed working directly with business partners to obtain information on exclusions for each card, inventory management and verifying store instructions were added.

R: This was a situation where I made sure no mistakes occurred which helped the company to continue its profitability in the gift card market. This helped the company generate over $10M in revenue in a six-month period.

Cut the Fluff, Please

When you write out your answers using **iRock S.T.A.R. Method™**, make sure to cut out the fluff. Only tell the meat of your answers. Don't beat around the bush. And don't get into nuances that made no difference in your ability to achieve the result.

Doing the above only elongates your answer. And, it also increases your chance of losing the attention of the interviewer(s).

In other words, chose your words carefully to answer the questions with power. Don't bore the interviewers with non-essential information. Wow, them with impactful facts instead.

All in all, I am proud of the **iRock S.T.A.R. Method**™ format. Use it with an awesome opening and closing statement. If you do, you will rock out the interview and land your dream job!

In the next chapter, I outline how to rock out your closing statement.

Use the area below to practice writing an example or two using the
iRock S.T.A.R Method™

_____

_____

_____

_____

_____

_____

_____

_____

Chapter Eight

Rock Out Your Closing Statement

> "An effective closing statement is your opportunity to "drop the mike" and exit stage left."
>
> — *Nickquolette Barrett, Career Development Strategist*

Rock Out Your Closing Statement

Most interviewers will end an interview by asking if you have any questions for them. This is your opportunity and queue to close the interview with a bang!

First, thank them for the opportunity to meet with you. If you have a few (legitimate) questions, then it's ok to ask them. Once you receive your answer(s), make sure you transition smoothly into your closing statement.

Questions to Ask, Only If Needed

I added this section as many of my clients ask what questions should they ask in an interview. I love when I get this question as it shows me that my clients understand the interview is a two-way street. Even though the interview is mostly about you. It is just as important to understand it's about the employer as well. Remember in chapter four when I spoke about "what if the job is not a good fit"?

Asking the potential employer questions the posting and/or recruiter did not answer for you, is a good idea. But, I warn you. Only ask questions if needed. Do not ask just for the sake of asking. The interviewer(s) will see right through it.

Also, refrain from asking investigative type questions you can find out on your own via the internet, company website, etc. Or even self-serving questions like *"How many vacation days do I get?"*

Instead, ask questions only the hiring managers and/or potential peers can answer. Be careful not to ask a closed ended question as these end in either a "yes" or "no" response. Instead, ask open ended questions as these tend to give more in-depth answers.

Here are a few questions you can ask.

- Can you tell me more about the day-to-day responsibilities of this job?
- How would you describe the company's culture?
- How would you describe the dynamics of the team or department?
- What are the biggest opportunities facing the company/department right now?
- What are the challenges for this role and within the department at this time?
- What are your expectations for this role during the first 90 days, 6 months', a year?
- What do you think are the most important qualities for someone to excel in this role?
- What is the typical career path for this role?

Note: Please do not ask salary or benefits questions during your first interview. Wait until you are in the final steps of the interview process. Once you understand the salary and benefits being offered, you can either move to negotiations or accept the offer.

Now for the BIG CLOSE

Let's go back to the attorney example in chapter six.

As an attorney finishes up their case, they have an opportunity to summarize what the jury has heard during the trial. They remind the jurors about key evidence presented. They go on to persuade them to adopt an interpretation favorable to their position. At this point, the attorney is advocating why the jurors should decide the case in their favor.

You as the interviewee will need to do the same thing. You want to advocate why the interviewer(s) should decide to hire you instead of a competitor. You must lay out your case and show them why you are the best candidate for the opportunity.

To close your interview, summarize your strengths, talents, abilities, and past accomplishments. This is your time to show how those skills will easily transfer to the opportunity before you. This is your opportunity *"drop the mike and exit stage left."*

When writing your closing statement, remember these points.

- Don't rehash the entire interview. Summarize instead.
- Make three statements why you are the best fit with examples from your interview.

The closing statement can both seal the deal and save the interview for you. Especially if you felt you did not do as well on the questions asked.

Ask for The Job

Last but not least, if this is your dream job please

ASK FOR THE JOB!

Yes, I said it. Ask for the job. Why not? There's nothing wrong with confidently asking for the job especially if it's one you want. What is not right is you do not ask. Or you ask arrogantly or desperately. To avoid either of these, end the interview with something like this:

"I'd really love the opportunity to work for you and this company. I really look forward to hearing from you soon."

Or

"I have done my research and feel this company and this opportunity is a right fit for me. I'd love to prove I am the right fit for the job. I look forward to hearing from you soon."

See. The statements above are not so bad, are they? No, they are not. They are easy to memorize and are not intimidating or too forward. The statements are safe and simple. They will not only show your true interest in the job, but they will elevate your interview a few notches.

Plus, the interviewer(s) will gain a level of respect for you being bold enough to ask. And, if you get the job, you start off with a heightened level of respect.

If you get the job after putting these tips into place, then it's time for you and I to work together to create an awesome career development strategy to get you to the next level!

On the next page, there are two examples of a closing statement I wrote for the same clients I wrote opening statements for in chapter six. Again, feel free to model your closing statement on either of these.

Closing Statement:

Panel: Well, iRock Client, this concludes the interview. Do you have any questions for us or is there anything you would like to add?

iRock Client: *(ask questions as needed)*

I would like to thank you for your time and for the opportunity to discuss my skills, knowledge, and abilities. This role is meant for me and I can assure you that I am prepared and ready for the task at hand.

- I have project experience that demonstrates my ability to collaborate with others to achieve department goals while leveraging the relationships I've built.
- I currently lead in an environment, where I influence others by coaching, mentoring and consulting. I do this with direct reports, peer leaders, upper leadership, and business partners.
- I collaborate in aligning the business needs with enterprise goals that create high yielding results.
- (I also wanted to share) in my preparation for today's interview, I have spoken with (insert anyone you spoke to) as well as took the initiative to (name any research you conducted)
- Lastly, I bring leadership maturity, integrity, and my passion for this role and therefore respectfully ask that you select me for this great opportunity.

Thank you again.

Closing:

Question: iRock client, do you have any questions for us? *(If you legitimately have questions, then ask. If you do not, then don't.)*

Yes/No (depending on if you do or not) but I would like to say that I can see myself as a great fit for your company and that your company culture lines up with my values of..... *(this has to come from your research of the company)*.

I feel my skills in accounts payable and the intricacies that go along with it, in addition to relationship building and being a great team player would line up with the position of _____. I would really love the opportunity to work with you and this company.

Thank you and I look forward to hearing from you.

Write a rough draft of your closing statement. The draft can be tweaked to fit each opportunity you are interviewing for.

Chapter Nine

Interview Question Types and How to Answer Them

> "Do not fabricate an interview answer. If you do and are not able to replicate it on the job, you might find yourself out of a job.
>
> *Nickquolette Barrett*
> Career Development Strategist

Interview Question Types and How to Answer Them

It is more fun to talk with someone who doesn't use long, difficult words but rather short, easy words like "What about lunch? – Winnie-the-Pooh

Practice typical interview questions and prepare answers in advance of the interview. Practice those answers. Better yet. If you can, invest in an interview prep session. The return on investment will be well worth it as you can use the skills learned in many areas of your career. If you invest in an interview prep session, make sure you find a company that offers a recorded version. Having a recorded version allows you to review your session as often as you like. iRock Résumés offers this service.

If an interview prep session is not in the budget, ask a mentor or friend to practice with you. Doing either of these, will be to your benefit. If you chose the latter option, please take note of your mistakes and work on them immediately. It will improve your readiness and build your confidence.

This chapter highlights different types of questions you may get in an interview.

I suggest you take time to develop strong real-life examples to showcase what you bring to the table. Do not fabricate your answers. If you do, and you are not able to replicate this result on the job, you might find yourself out of a job. Therefore, put in some serious thought into your answers. Go to your bank of answers discussed in chapter seven. You will be surprised by how many examples you actually have.

Your examples should include competencies to convey your ability to do the job.

A great way to do this is to:

1. tear the job description apart and pick out the competencies
2. pull from your bank of real examples that align with the competencies identified in the job description

3. compare the job description to your résumé
4. combine the best of both worlds to create an awesome interview answer

And, in your preparation, use the **iRock S.T.A.R. Method™** as you formulate your answers.

There are different types of interview questions. The three most common are:

- Behavioral / Situational
- Competency Based
- Hypothetical

The Behavioral / Situational Question

Interviewer(s) use the behavioral/situational question to determine your past behaviors in certain work experiences to predict what type of behavior you will display in the future. It helps the interviewer(s) to discover how you will behave or react to specific work situations within their company.

Typical behavioral/situational questions are:

Tell me about a time when you worked with a difficult team member. How did you handle it?

➤ With this question, pick an experience where you were the hero. Show how you either mentored, befriended, encouraged, or coached the person to work better with the team.

We all make mistakes we wish we could take back. Tell me about a time you wish you handled a situation differently. What you would do if you have the opportunity to handle it differently today?

➤ This is a tricky question. I recommend thinking of a time when you were able to rectify a situation. Doing this changes it from a "wish

I could've should've" answer, to you "did" something to make it better. How you behaved is what they are looking for. Show you behaved in a way to make the situation better.

Tell me of a situation where you met resistance introducing a new idea, concept, or procedure to a team or work group. What did you do? What was the outcome?

> In this example think of a time where you were able to ease the resistance of a group. You want to display your people and persuasive skills by transforming mindsets. Show how you were able to gain insight into their minds and help them embrace the new idea or direction.

> This kind of question helps the interviewer determine how intelligent a candidate is. It is a tool used to place a candidate in a situation while providing an avenue for him or her to be observed. Practical knowledge of the job is needed. But to actually perform it, is the key to this type of question.

Tell me about a time you helped resolve a dispute between others?

> This question is to check if you have problem solving or influence skills needed on every job under the sun. It is always good to pick from a more recent incident. Make it specific to a strategy you used to resolve a situation. Emphasize the strategy part of your response as this elevates your answer.

The Competency Based Question

Competency-based interviews are more systematic. Each question targets a specific skill or competency. The interviewer(s) are looking for your ability to show through past experiences your aptitude of a specific competency needed to do the job.

Behavioral and situational questions can overlap. However, the competency will be the main focal point of the question. You will be asked to explain specific circumstances demonstrating the competency. You will need to have concrete examples.

Most job descriptions have the competencies listed. It would be wise to have examples ready for each competency listed.

Typical competency based questions are:

Describe a time when you had to deal with a major change in your work environment, work process and/or job duties. How did you respond and prepare for the change?

- ➤ Competency: Adaptability – alters the approach as the situation demands. Works effectively within a variety of situations and with various individuals and groups.

Sometimes it's a challenge to get everything on your to-do list done. Tell me about a time your responsibilities became overwhelming. What did you do? How did you resolve feeling overwhelmed?

- ➤ Competency: Time-management – the act or process of planning and exercising conscious control over the amount of time spent on specific activities to increase effectiveness, efficiency, or productivity.

Give an example of a time when you had to explain something complex to an upset customer. How did you handle this situation? What was the outcome?

- ➤ Competency: Communication – the ability to express ideas and views clearly, confidently and concisely in speech tailoring your response and style to the audience.

Tell me about a time you solved a complex problem. What was the problem? What were the steps you took to solve it? What was the outcome? If it was not successful, what would you have done differently?

> ➢ Competency: Problem-solving skills relate to your ability to identify issues, obstacles, and opportunities and then develop and implement effective solutions.

Tell me about a time you showed intiative in your role? Describe the situation and the steps you took.

> ➢ Competency: Initiative – Recognizes what needs to be done and accomplishes it proactively.

Give a specific example in which you were asked to complete an assignment or project with little to no direction. What steps did you take? What was the outcome of the assignment/project?

> ➢ Competency: Resourcefulness – identifies quality resources, information, and materials needed to complete a task.

Give me a specific example in which you were faced with a difficult deadline to meet. What did you do? What was the outcome?

> ➢ Competency: Work Ethic – displays values which contribute to a shared focus, exhibits high level of commitment, is motivated to achieve, and demonstrate responsible behavior.

Hypothetical Question

This type of question is based on an idea or suggestion about what might happen or might be true. It is not always based on a real situation, although it could be. It is also used to put the interviewee on the spot. The questions are directed to the character, background, tendency, and more of the interviewee.

The hypothetical question is used to:

- see how a candidate reacts under pressure
- check your response to a given event
- predict and/or determine what might you do if the situation happened
- see how you think and develop your answers based on a hypothetical situation
- see how you would behave in the same "hypothetical" situation

Typical hypothetical questions are:

If you were hiring a person for this job, what would you look for?

> This question is an opportunity to discuss how a person with your skill set is the best fit for the job. You must be careful that your response is related to what will be needed in the job. You will need to articulate you have at least 95% of the requirements. This will show the interviewer(s) you can become productive pretty quickly if hired.

What would you do if a customer came storming into the office blaming you for everything that went wrong with the services they received?

> This is an opportunity to show how you deal with a difficult customer. In answering this question, make sure to show how you can calm the customer down and then go into problem solving mode.

What would you do if you knew a co-worker who was stealing from the company? This co-worker happened to be your best friend.

> This question is all about honesty and integrity. Employment or friendship. Your choice.

Fact Finding Questions

Below are basic questions interviewers ask to get a better feel for who you are. The answers to these questions can tell what kind of person you are – professionally and personally.

Typical fact finding questions are:

Tell me about yourself.

- ➤ This is where you give them your awesome opening statement we discussed in Chapter 8. Refer to it if needed.

What do you know about our organization?

- ➤ This shows the interviewer if you did any research. This is where you discuss products or services, reputation, philanthropic efforts, goals, vision, mission, history, or philosophy. No need to hit on all the above, just touch on some of them in a concise format.

- ➤ During your research, write a snippet of what you know about the company in your own words. This will show you took the time to learn about your potential employer. Don't overwhelm the interviewer(s) by regurgitating their website. It could be overkill.

- ➤ Give your answer a positive tone. Start your answer something like this: *"In my job search, I've investigated several companies. Yours is one of the few that interested me for these reasons..."* End this question by making it clear you wish to learn more.

Why should I hire you?

- ➤ This question is thrown at you to make you fully aware that you are on the hot seat. It is a question to check how you respond to pressure right from the onset.

- Although this question appears to paint the interviewer as a difficult person. It equally gives you a golden opportunity to display your potential to the employer.
- Take a deep breath and gather your thoughts. Remember, you prepared for this. Go right into the answer by discussing what you can do for the company to take them to the next level.

Why are you leaving (did you leave) your present (last) job?

- Be brief, to the point, and as honest as you can without hurting yourself or your current or past employer. If you were laid off in an across-the-board cut back, say so. Otherwise, tell them the move is your decision, the result of your actions. You can even discuss the desire for better opportunities and their company provides those opportunities.
- Do not mention personality conflicts with people on the job and most of all, your former boss.
- The interviewer may spend some time probing you on this issue. Especially if it is clear the company terminated you. At this point, the *"we agreed to disagree"* approach may be helpful. Keep in mind, they may check your references.
- Don't concoct a story for the sake of an interview, as the last thing you want to be labeled as dishonest. So please BE HONEST!

On the scale of 1- 10 how would you rate yourself?

- There is a tendency for you to respond selfishly, but be truthful. It's safe to say your range is between 8 to 9 because you leave room to grow and learn. Make your statement with all sincerity. Stay away from saying you are a solid 10 unless you have mastered all you need in your career.

What have you done to improve your knowledge in the last few years?

> This question is used to check how serious you are in pursuing self-development. You can answer by indicating job related activities like special projects, and/or stretch assignments. Be sure to include industry specific or general business books read, seminars attended, information acquired, and classes taken. If you are not doing anything like the above, get busy. Self-development is beneficial.

Are you a good leader? If so, why?

> If you are applying for a leadership position, saying you know how to lead is not enough. You need to be able to show your leadership skills in your responses and with examples. The interviewers want to know how well you can lead people. Show you are principled and disciplined, yet understanding and fair. If you are not a leader by title, use examples where you were either seen as a leader on a team or led certain projects.

What motivates you?

> Everyone has something that motivates them to achieve their best. It varies from one individual to another. Whatever you choose as a means of motivation, make sure your response is positive.

Why did you choose this particular career path?

> Think through this answer very carefully. Discuss your passions, interests, intrigues, and/or the like. Never discuss money at this point because it may give an illusion you are only in it for the money.

> Base your reason on wanting to use your skill set as a way of career fulfillment. Ok to say you choose to be in the field because you are either passionate about it or very talented at it. If you believe it is a way you can fulfill your purpose, say it.

What motivates you to work hard?

- The first thing you should put into consideration is your passion. It drives you to want to do more. You can mention your desire to achieve. You can also say you have a sense of fulfillment from any role you are in.
- Obviously, results bring rewards. Equally mention material reward from achieving goals such as increased salary, bonuses, and benefits. But, don't belabor the point. Again, you don't want money to be a driving force in your desire to work for a company.

What are your long-term goals?

- Refer to the research phase of your job search. Say something like *"In a company like yours, I would like to..."* and give the reasons why based on your research. If you see this as a long-term partnership, then say so.

    Overall, while interviewing can be nerve-wrecking, it can also be a source of confidence. Confidence in knowing you get a chance to articulate your skills, abilities, and talents in a concise and impactful way. The entire process is an exchange of information – one to another. It's a way to determine if the candidate and the company are a good match.

Chapter Ten

What to Do After the Interview

> "Follow up immediately after an interview to keep your name top of mind."
>
> — Nickquolette Barrett, Career Development Strategist

What to Do After the Interview

You just came out of the interview and are full of expectation to secure your dream job. You feel you knocked it out the part – awesome opening, great answers, and a memorable closing. You feel on top of the world! To keep this feeling, it will be imperative to stay connected with the employer.

Stay connected by sending a thank you letter/email within 24 hours. This is a sure way to keep your name top of mind with the decision maker(s). You can put a two or three sentences in it to remind them of the skills, abilities, and talents you can bring to the job opportunity.

Refer to the list of names I mentioned in chapter two where I suggested you get the correct spelling of the interviewer(s) names. If you prepared thank you letters in advance, then you are on the ball! I highly recommend sending a thank you letter as it's more personal than an email. If you do both, even better.

Here's an example of why doing this is important.

A friend of mine left a management position at a company to relocate with her husband. She found a company she wanted to work for and decided to apply for a lower position just to get her foot in the door.

The friend walked into the interview and articulated her skills, talents, and abilities. She left the interview and followed up with the decision makers with thank you letters and email. Unfortunately, she did not get the lower level job.

However, the recruiter had a management position she qualified for. He called her up and offered it to her. You talk about SCORE! She had no idea she would even be considered since did not apply for the position. She has since flourished at the company and has risen to an even higher management position. Who knew! The gold is found in the follow up. Your goal is to maximize every opportunity to sell yourself, even in the thank you letter.

Connecting with the interviewer(s) and recruiters, even if you do not get the job, gives you an opportunity to make professional contacts. When another job opportunity becomes available, having those connections will be valuable in being considered for it.

How Many Times Should I Follow Up?

I'm glad you asked! The initial follow up should be immediate – within 24 hours as stated above. If you don't hear anything in a week, follow up again. If you don't hear anything in a week after that, follow up one more time. Each time you follow up, continue to express your interest in the role.

However, while waiting for a response to one job, please do not sit around waiting. Continue your job search. Why? Because companies make changes all the time. The role could no longer be available, the recruiter or hiring manager has been reassigned, ill, or simply no longer work there. Life happens which means yours should not stop by waiting on someone else. Keep it moving by keeping your job search alive until you land the right opportunity for you.

I included a thank you letter example at the end of this chapter. Feel free to use it as a template when creating your own.

iRock Client, MBA, CPA

Dynamic finance leadership professional ready to implement strategies to achieve your bottom line goals

123-456-7891
City, State Zip Code
iRockClient@email.com
www.linkedin.com/in/iRockClient

{Date}

{Employer Contact Information}

Re: {Job posting ID or Name of Position}

Thank you for taking the time to meet with me to discuss the {name of job here} opportunity.

As stated, I pride myself on becoming an asset to any {company or organization} that I am affiliated with. I would love the opportunity to do the same for your {company or organization} as your new {name of job here}.

I am a self-starter and seek out ways to make significant contributions. I will use my relationship building and creative problem-solving skills to achieve results. Also, I am a financial leadership professional par excellent. I have the fortitude to bring excellence to your organization.

Again, thank you for taking the time to consider me for this great opportunity. I look forward to developing a beneficial partnership.

Sincerely,

iRock Client, MBA, CPA

Write a rough draft of a thank you letter using the example as a template. Tweak it to add your information.

Appendix I

Final Thoughts

Be sure to familiarize yourself with the job posting and the résumé you submitted for the job. This is extremely important if you use various versions of your résumé.

Review it several times and for several days before the interview. You don't want to be caught off guard when answering a question derived from the résumé. This could be the death of the interview and your dream job.

Taking the time to prepare for the interview will be beneficial to you and the interviewer. And, it can be the key to you hearing the words:

You're hired!

****

This will round out this book. It has been a pleasure writing it. I urge you to put the tips to good use and watch what happens. And, when you do, drop me a line to let me know about your success. I love hearing from my readers. And who knows, your testimony just might make it into a future book.

Finally, if this book helped you, please share with someone who can use these tips. Getting folks back to work and/or into a better opportunity is my ultimate mission.

Thanks for reading!

After reading this book, what will your next steps be? Have questions about your personal situation? List them here and give me a call.
I would be happy to assist.

_____

_____

_____

_____

_____

_____

_____

_____

_____

_____

Thank you so much for purchasing my book!

I am passionate about helping serious career professionals, just like you, understand they are more than just an employee. You are in fact your own corporation, your own brand, and your own CEO.

My personal creed is:

- ❖ If I can help 1 person elevate their career by a thought provoking statement, then I have succeeded.
- ❖ If I can help 10 people elevate their career with my voice, then I have succeeded.
- ❖ If I can help 100s people elevate their career by my personal services, then I have succeeded.
- ❖ If I can help 1000s of people elevate their career with the written word, then I have succeeded.

In essence, I work to change your mindset from employee to business owner within the structure of corporate America. You don't have to be an entrepreneur in the sense of owning an actual business. However, you do have to see yourself as an entrepreneur of your own brand and value in the job marketplace. You are a business of one! I can show you how to run your "business" to be an impact in your career and get results.

Contact iRock Résumés to get started!

iRock Client Testimonials

"I would highly recommend Nickquolette to anyone. She is great at what she does. Very professional, personal and hands on. What makes her so good is that she really loves what she does. She helped me with my résumé me and I love it. Nickquolette helped me prepare for an interview. After the interview session, I had all the confidence I needed to go in there and knock them out. She has a great spirit and knows what she is doing." – *Felicia McQurter – Joint Interest Accountant*

Part 1. "This is so awesome. Just by the way. I think this is an awesome service you provide. Especially for people like myself. I'm going to send many people your way. I look forward to working with you again. I truly appreciate you."

Part 2. "Hi! I got the job! Yaaaaay!!! Thank you so much for all your help with preparing me for the interview. The interview feedback said I was confident, yet humble. I thought because that was the holy spirit shining through me. God was near my friend. – *Lakita Wheat, MBA – recently promoted Team Manager*

Part 1. "Nickquolette has been very helpful throughout the process of re-writing my résumé. Her keen insights and years of experience redesigning résumé have resulted in an excellent résumé. She gave invaluable advice during the interview preparation session. I recommend her to anyone who wants to land their dream job." – *Bhargava Rohit Sagi, Industrial Engineer*

Part 2. "Hey Nickquolette, I hope you're doing well! I wanted to inform you that I got a job in California and I move here a couple of weeks ago. Thanks for all your help during my job search. – *Best regards, Bhargava.*"

Part 1. "Hi Nickquolette – Thank you for meeting with my son today and for all that you have done to help him. It was kind of you to send me this summary with next steps. It is great that he will be ready to submit some internship applications at the end of the week before he returns to college. I know that he will be much better prepared for the career fair and interviews too. Take care!

Part 2. "Nickquolette – I just had to tell you that your résumé and interview prep worked!! I'm glad to report that my son got an internship and the interviewers were impressed with his résumé and interview skills. Thank you so much and I'm going to make sure I report back to the NAPW (National Association of Professional Women) to let them know how awesome you are. Thank you! – *Ruth McGuffey – Non-profit Leader-Education Sector and mother of a college student*

About the Author

Nickquolette Barrett is a Career Development Strategist & CEO/Founder of iRock Development Solutions, LLC d/b/a iRock Résumés – *Land the job of your dreams and create a career that rocks!*

Nickquolette was born and raised in Chicago, IL. She and her family relocated to Texas in 2008. She has been happily married to Senior Pastor, Rev. Dr. Irvin L. Barrett since 1994 and they have a beautiful daughter, Nadia MyAngel.

Nickquolette has worked in corporate America since 1994 and received her first promotion to leadership in 1999. Her vast career experience includes operations using six-sigma lean principles, diversity & inclusion, corporate training, advertising, marketing, corporate sponsorships, customer service, employee development/advancement, and sales. She is often selected for special projects, mentoring, facilitation, moderating opportunities.

Over the years, she has created numerous successful career development strategies that have worked in advancing the careers of others. With her success, she decided to launch iRock Development Solutions, LLC dba iRock Résumés.

Nickquolette loves to create and organize conferences, workshops, and seminars. She is also an engaging speaker. Her passion for helping people get unstuck and create a rockin' career is felt when she speaks. She brings a fresh unique, and real perspective with sensitivity and a side of humor.

As a Career Development Strategist, Expert Résumé Writer, and Interview Prep Coach, Nickquolette's goal is to fulfill her company's mission by taking it to the masses. You can help spread her mission by connecting with her on social media and sharing with others.

iRock Résumés mission is to:

- ✓ turn every job applicant into a viable job candidate
- ✓ help shift client's mindset from employee to CEO of their career destiny
- ✓ to help clients find financial security for themselves and their family
- ✓ to help the employer gain an engaged employee focused on getting results

We equip candidates with the tools needed to land, keep, and create an intentional and fulfilling career.

Below, you will find contact information on how to hire Nickquolette to assist with your career development needs and to speak at your next event.

Also, consider joining iRock's VIP mailing list to receive tips on résumé writing, interview prep, career development and more at www.irockresumes.com. You will be the first to know of special promotions, events, and upcoming books.

Connect with Nickquolette

- Website: irockresumes.com
- LinkedIn/in/Nickquolette Barrett
- Twitter @irockresumes
- Instagram @irockresumes

- Facebook @iRock Résumés
- YouTube: Nickquolette Barrett – "Nickquolette's Career Musings"

For bulk orders, contact irock@irockresumes.com and place put "Bulk Order" in the subject line.

Made in the USA
Columbia, SC
07 March 2019